blasta (blastə) *adj* From the Irish language, meaning delicious, tasty, appetising. Rhymes with pasta.

Blasta Books are to cookbooks what street food is to restaurants: a fun, accessible and affordable way to eat exciting food.

At Blasta Books, we believe that the two things that connect everyone, everywhere, are food and stories. If you draw a Venn diagram with **food** in one circle and **stories** in the other, **connection** is what's in the middle where the circles overlap. Food and stories are what we all have in common, no matter who we are or where we're from.

That's why we're working to make more room at the table, one bite and one book at a time. Pull up a chair and dig in.

samba

A Celebration of Brazilian Cuisine

Giselle Makinde

contents

Introduction 1
Brazilian cuisine: A dance between three nations 6
The Brazilian pantry 8

Cassava: The queen of Brazilian cuisine 10
Biscoito de polvilho (tapioca crackers) 12
Pão de queijo (cheese bread) 14
Bobó de camarão (shrimp stew with cassava and coconut milk) 16

Corn: The golden grain 18
Cuscuz paulista (savoury cornmeal cake) 20
Cuscuz nordestino (steamed corn couscous) 22
Bolo de fubá com calda de goiabada
(cornmeal cake with guava sauce) 24
Curau de milho (sweetcorn custard) 26

Beans: A Brazilian staple 28
Feijoada (black bean stew) 30
Banana frita (fried banana) 33
Farofa 33
Couve (sautéed collard greens) 33
Feijão tropeiro (cattle drovers' beans) 34
Baião de dois (rice and beans with meat and cheese) 36

Banana: Brazil's beloved fruit 38

Bolo de banana (banana bread) 40

Carne louca de casca de banana (pulled banana peels) 42

Cartola (banana with cheese) 44

Coconut: Sweet and savoury versatility 46

Moqueca de peixe com pirão (Brazilian fish stew) 48

Quindim (coconut custard) 50

Cocada (coconut sweets) 51

Carne seca: Brazilian dried beef 52

Escondidinho de carne seca (Brazilian shepherd's pie) 54

Jabá com jerimum (dried beef with pumpkin) 56

Paçoca de carne seca (dried beef and cassava crumble) 58

Sugarcane: Our sweet heritage 60

Caipirinha 62

Brazilian birthday party sweets 64

Pastel (fried pastry) 66

Congelamento de Alimentos

introduction

I don't remember ever hearing my mom or grandmother say 'I love you' out loud, but they said it every day in their own way, through every dish they cooked. That's how love was served in our home: on a plate. I've inherited that, so if I invite you over for Sunday lunch or Friday night dinner, know this: it means eu te amo (I love you). Food is my love language, and cooking is how I care for the people in my life.

All my best childhood memories are tied to my mom or grandmother in the kitchen, preparing meals for our family. Yet the food in my childhood is hard to define. It was a mix of Portuguese-inspired, Brazilian and everything in between, from Ofélia's TV shows to the culinary magazines my mom collected. If I asked my mom, 'What's for lunch?', the answer was always the same: 'Food.' And dinner? 'Same as lunch: food! Eat it!' Being fussy about food was simply not allowed.

My father often joked that it was only after marrying my mom that he learned to eat anything other than rice topped with minced meat. The variety of dishes and ingredients she cooked for us was unusual for the time, each meal a new combination. Rice and beans, the daily staple in most Brazilian households, weren't regulars at our table. Instead, we had pies, stews, vegetables, salads, fish, meat. As a young teenager, summer holidays meant trips to Brazil's Northeast, where I discovered the beauty of its cuisine: feijão de corda, moqueca, manteiga de garrafa, carne de sol and more. At home, I also tasted a bit of the Northeast in the food my grandmother and aunties prepared for family parties. I still vividly remember my aunt's birthday when she served bobó de camarão (see page 16). It was the first time I tasted the dish, and it became my favourite one of all.

On my mom's side of the family, gatherings were more formal. As the only children among adults, my brothers and I had to mind our manners, especially when it came to trying the different dishes. The dinners carried a certain ceremony, and that ritual always held a special enchantment for me. On my father's side, it was the opposite: loud, fun, overflowing with cousins whose names I could barely keep straight. The food was improvised. If more people showed up, you just stretched what you had. Add rice to the pasta, add water to the beans, and suddenly there was enough for everyone. Christmas highlighted these contrasts even more. On my mom's side, bacalhau (dried cod) reigned over turkey, while on my dad's side, the table overflowed with all sorts of dishes. And the best part? Samba playing all night long after the gifts were exchanged.

Dining out was a rare luxury, reserved for birthdays or anniversaries, and even then, it didn't really happen until we were older. So we brought the fun of eating out into our home instead. Saturday evenings meant my father taking over the kitchen to make his famous pizza on bread, always with music in the background. Sundays meant long lunches at Vó Maria and Vô José's house (my mom's parents) and afternoons at Vó Lourdes and Vô João's (my dad's parents), where eating bread with salted Aviação butter (Brazilians over 40 will remember!), shared with cousins, was a staple.

As kids, our birthdays were always celebrated at home. My mom spent days preparing everything: baking the cake, making brigadeiros (page 64), cooking sanduíche de carne louca and savoury pastries like empadas (her empada remains the best I've ever had). I remember the excitement in the air, the balloons in the living room, my father carefully recording a playlist on a cassette tape, and me and my sister helping my mom roll brigadeiros and other sweets in sprinkles the night before the party. We'd wear new clothes bought just for the occasion, clothes that would become our going-out outfits until we outgrew them. The preparation was better than the party itself. We would play with our neighbours, family and friends, dance, run and laugh. By the end of the day, we were exhausted but happy. My mom, though, was still in her apron and her red scarf, running around to make sure everyone was fed. I don't remember her ever sitting down to enjoy the party.

When stand-up freezers became popular in the 1990s, my mom was the first in our neighbourhood to get one. She taught herself everything about freezing food and how different ingredients responded to different techniques, and soon she started teaching others. Our living room turned into a classroom in the afternoons, with up to 15 women learning how to save time and effort in the kitchen. I still have her class book filled with recipes, *Congelamento de Alimentos* (*Freezing Food*), with a cover designed by my father. Sharing a photo of it in my own book (it's on the previous page) is a real full-circle moment.

But I also remember watching her struggle to sell her food. She made frozen meals, baked birthday cakes and cooked weekly meals to sell to our neighbours to try to earn some money. Back then, being a cook didn't seem glamorous or exciting. It wasn't the celebrated profession it is today. From my point of view, it was just hard work, done out of love and necessity (that part remains the same).

My mom, Ana Maria Pereira Gonçalves, and my grandmother are my inspirations when it comes to cooking. I can't quite remember what made me start thinking about being a cook, but around my second year studying tourism at university, the idea of switching courses and diving into the culinary world emerged. Still, my mom encouraged me to finish what I had started – having a diploma was important to open doors for my future. I was just 20 when I completed my course. One week after presenting my final project, my mother passed away after bravely fighting breast cancer for years. A few months later, I got my first job in a restaurant called Brooklin in São Paulo.

my culinary journey

Being a chef was still a relatively new concept in the early 1990s in Brazil. At that time, French chefs had just begun arriving in the country, bringing with them classical techniques and a new perspective on cooking. They started using local Brazilian ingredients in more refined, modern ways. With time and through magazines and media, the title 'chef' began to carry prestige. It sounded far more glamorous than simply being a cook.

I didn't know what mirepoix was, or concassé, or any of the French terms that are so common in the cheffing world. When I walked into my first restaurant kitchen back in 2000, I knew only one thing: being in a kitchen made me happy. I was like a kid stepping into a classroom for the first time, eager to learn how to write. I had the passion, but I was starting from scratch and ready to soak up everything I could.

That was me for the next year – learning techniques, developing skills, growing as a person and as a chef. Then, one year later, I was accepted into a culinary programme called Cozinheiro Básico at Senac Águas de São Pedro. It was a hotel-school where I spent six intense months learning how to cut, cook and prepare everything from vegetables to meat. Apart from feijoada every Saturday, the focus was on international and French cuisine and base sauces, and the techniques and classics of European cooking. Brazilian cuisine wasn't part of the curriculum. It wasn't even a module.

After finishing the course, I went back to the first restaurant I had worked at. But this time, I wasn't a rookie. I had a diploma, skills and confidence. I was put in the pastry section, my first real assignment as a professional.

But do you want to know the best part of working there? It wasn't the techniques I learned or the dishes I plated. It was what happened after the shift ended. Around 2 or 3 a.m., we would head to a tiny boteco in Itaim Bibi, a hole-in-the-wall place that served the best baião de dois, always topped with a perfectly fried egg. It wasn't glamorous – just a bunch of cooks who spent the whole day preparing duck confit and cassoulet – but when it came time to feed ourselves, we craved something simple and deeply comforting. Those late-night meals weren't just about the food; they were about connection. About grounding ourselves in something familiar and soul-warming. At that little boteco, over bowls of baião de dois, we recharged. It was food that fed our souls. It gave us the strength to go home, grab a few hours of sleep and do it all over again.

That time taught me something that no cooking course ever could: the real power of food isn't in the technique or the presentation. It's in its ability to comfort, to connect and to say 'I love you' without using words.

From that first restaurant, I moved on to others, always with the same group of chefs. That was our rhythm: opening new places, building menus, hiring a team, getting it all to work, then moving on to the next one. For about four years, that was my life. But eventually, I felt the need to finally learn English, which took me to El Paso, Texas, where I lived with an American family, Pat and Larry Garcia and their daughters. It was there that I had my first taste of entrepreneurship. From Pat's kitchen, I started baking brownies and pumpkin cheesecakes, selling them to the staff at the school where Pat worked. That soon led to catering a few events at the local church, which sparked my entrepreneurial spirit.

Back in Brazil, I opened my first production kitchen, supplying goods to companies and organising coffee breaks. From there, I opened my first coffeeshop inside a women's clothing store, where I baked pão de queijo, my mother's delicious empadas and one of the best-sellers: escondidinho de carne seca (a Brazilian shepherd's pie; see page 54). Another opportunity came along, and I took on a second coffeeshop inside an orchard's store.

But it wasn't all flowers and rainbows; far from it. I didn't know much about running a business, and my lack of experience quickly turned into a hard lesson. Eventually, I had to close both coffeeshops and the production kitchen. But when a door closes, a window opens. That's when I found myself teaching at Senac, one of the top culinary schools in Brazil.

I taught teenagers, ages 13 to 17, from a favela in Jaguaré, São Paulo, how to cook. For almost six months, I worked with one group of teens in the morning and another in the afternoon, teaching them everything from how to boil an egg to preparing more complex dishes, breads and desserts. The excitement in their eyes when a recipe worked, and the joy of watching them savour their hard-earned creations, made it one of the most rewarding experiences food has brought into my life.

I became deeply attached to them, almost like a big mama bear. Coincidentally, I got pregnant during that period, which only amplified my maternal instincts. Watching their pride in learning, growing and creating gave me an overwhelming sense of fulfilment. Coming from such poor backgrounds, many of them had little access to opportunities, and I felt that through food I was offering them not just skills, but a sense of direction and possibility. The first group was so successful that they ran the course again, then again. I ended up teaching teenagers for three years.

Fast forward eight years, and I decided to move to Ireland with the hope of a new beginning. I didn't know anyone there, but I knew my chef skills would be my greatest asset. After all, no matter where you go in the world, everyone eats. That gave me the confidence that I would be able to find a job. And I did, but I also felt my entrepreneurial spirit rushing back. During the pandemic, I started a sustainable ice cream business called Cream of the Crop, using perfectly good ingredients, mostly fruits, that would have otherwise gone to waste. Over its four years of operation, we saved more than 50 tons of food from going to waste.

Only now, as I write this, do I realise that, without even noticing, I have been walking my mother's path, following her footsteps through food and teaching and continuing the journey she began. The knowledge I've gathered along the way, combined with the memories my mom gave me, has carried me farther than I could have imagined. In a way, I made the opposite journey of my grandfather, who left Portugal for Brazil in the late 1930s in search of a new beginning and built a family there. Decades later, I left Brazil for Ireland, also in search of a new beginning. And I found it, through food, which has always been my bridge between the past and the future.

let's samba!

Living abroad either makes you feel closer to your home country or disconnected from it. In my case, I felt disconnected. Nobody leaves their country when everything is working well or it's perfect, and I moved to Ireland without looking back. I needed a fresh start. But every time I cooked rice with beans, farofa, vinaigrette and sausage, I smiled. Through food, memories of my family and happier times came rushing back. It was instant connection. Brazilians often give more value to products and ideas when they come from abroad, but once we are the ones living abroad, patriotism takes over. The longing for what we no longer have becomes a powerful reminder of where we come from and who we still are.

My idea for this book started from the expression 'Vai dar samba!', a popular Brazilian phrase that means something is going to work out. We use it to celebrate when things come together. Samba is a vibrant and unique rhythm, and so is our food. This book is also my way of reconnecting with my heritage and a legacy for my son and for other Brazilians born and raised outside of Brazil. I want the world to discover the richness of our cuisine, to see that it deserves not just recognition but a rightful place among the greats of global gastronomy.

Brazilian food is more than a list of ingredients – it's happiness, sunshine and dance. It's loud, it's vibrant and it's meant to be shared. You don't eat Brazilian food alone. You cook it together and you share it around the table, and suddenly it's a party.

That's exactly the atmosphere I want to create with this book, so when you're cooking these recipes, call your friends, turn up the music (check out my Samba playlist on Spotify!), sway to the rhythm, shake up a caipirinha or just crack open a Guaraná and samba!

Brazilian cuisine

a dance between three nations

I often say that we Brazilians don't have a typical face. We're a mix of peoples, a beautiful blend of cultures that deu samba! I'm a good example of this mix. Look at my names: Portuguese (Pereira), African (Makinde, a Nigerian/Yoruba name) and Indigenous (Gonçalves, a name given to my grandfather, as Indigenous people traditionally didn't have surnames). Brazilian people and Brazilian food were born at the same time, rooted in Indigenous knowledge, shaped by Portuguese influence and enriched by African resilience. Our food tells that story.

Most of the information we have from that time comes from letters written by travellers who arrived in Brazil, as well as from the Jesuits, who aimed to convert Indigenous people to Catholicism. Their diet was based on whatever they could find in nature: cassava, corn, potatoes, peanuts, fruits, roots, fish and birds. The queen, cassava, was normally ground into flour and often eaten with chilli, a staple at every meal.

Everything changed as soon as the Portuguese arrived on the shores of what is today Porto Seguro (Bahia) in 1500. Portuguese sailors dressed in fancy clothes, using forks and knives, drinking wine, speaking a different language and sleeping in beds must have been a shock to Indigenous people. The first foods they ever tried from Portugal were bread, cooked fish, sweets, honey and overripe figs. It was not love at first bite.

Portugal played an important role in the global spread of ingredients during the Age of Exploration from the 15th to the 17th century. Spices were taken from India to all over Europe, coconut trees from the Cape Verde islands to Brazil and the Caribbean, and tomatoes and potatoes from South America to Europe. Meanwhile, cassava, chillies and cashews from Brazil crossed the ocean to Africa and India. Portugal brought sugarcane, bananas, coconuts and mangoes. The global food landscape changed because of Portuguese people.

Historical documents also say that during the reign of Dom João VI (1808–1821), he used the botanical gardens in Rio de Janeiro to test crops from all over the world.

Whatever adapted well to the Brazilian soil and climate was then cultivated and spread across the country.

The Indigenous people didn't have breakfast, lunch or dinner – they simply ate whenever they felt hungry. They would hunt, gather and eat right away. Since Brazil doesn't have a harsh winter like Europe, there was no need to store food for months. Food was consumed as needed, fresh from nature. The Portuguese introduced the concept of mealtimes and the tradition of associating specific dishes with certain days of the week. It's a habit that remains strong in São Paulo, Rio de Janeiro and other states.

The limited access to European ingredients created the perfect environment to shape what we now call Brazilian food. Wheat was scarce, so cake recipes were adapted using cornmeal or cassava flour. Almonds gave way to peanuts and coconut. But the most important addition was eggs. Ignored by Africans and unknown to Indigenous people, Portuguese women changed the game when they showed the Indigenous women the multiples uses of eggs. Cunhãs (the Tupi word for women) began learning the art of Portuguese cooking, and naturally they mixed that with what they knew in relation to taste and techniques.

Around this time, salt, sugar and fat, which weren't part of African or Indigenous diets, began to appear. Cattle, chicken and turkey started arriving from Portuguese ships. Indigenous people weren't big fans of chicken, and neither were most Africans. But beef? Oh, yes.

The dried meat and fish introduced by the Portuguese, combined with the different types of cassava flour and corn flour, is what made the long travels around Brazil possible. Have you seen the size of the country?! Can you imagine how hard it must have been to populate this huge area and take food to all those places? Like in many other cultures around the world, finding ways to preserve food was a matter of survival and the use of salt to cure meat gave rise to one of our most iconic ingredients: dried beef.

As the Portuguese influence expanded, each region began to develop its own recipes and food traditions. Enslaved Africans from different nations brought their culinary knowledge with them. Banana and dendê oil were among the most significant African contributions to Brazilian food.

Over the course of Brazil's history, different economic cycles – the sugar cycle, cocoa cycle, coffee cycle, gold cycle and diamond cycle – helped shape the country's culture, but they also transformed the economy. Then, in the 20th century, the arrival of immigrants from Italy, Japan, Germany and elsewhere added even more flavour to the cultural melting pot we call Brazil. The food that emerged during those times, combined with the culinary influences I grew up with, forms the foundation of the recipes you'll find in this book.

the Brazilian pantry

These ingredients are the heart and soul of many Brazilian dishes.

AZEITE DE DENDÊ (RED PALM OIL)
A bright orange, earthy oil derived from the African oil palm. It has a unique flavour that can't be replaced and is essential in Afro-Brazilian dishes like moqueca and bobó de camarão.

BIQUINHO PEPPER
Native to Brazil, this small, teardrop-shaped chilli can be yellow or red and is mildly sweet and tangy. It's often pickled and served as a side or garnish.

CACHAÇA
Brazil's national spirit, distilled from fresh sugarcane juice (unlike rum, which is usually made from molasses). It's the star of the caipirinha cocktail, but is also used in marinades, desserts and flambéed dishes. Substitute: Vodka.

CARNE SECA, CARNE DE SOL AND CHARQUE
These are all types of preserved meat. Carne seca is salted and sun-dried, carne de sol is lightly salted and air-dried (it's less intense than carne seca) and charque is heavily salted and dried (it's more common in the south). They are used in feijoada, escondidinho and baião de dois.

COUVE-MANTEIGA
A leafy green similar to collard greens but thinner and more tender, couve-manteiga is a staple in Brazilian kitchens, especially as a side for feijoada. It's typically shredded very finely before being quickly sautéed with garlic and oil. Substitute: York cabbage.

FARINHA DE MANDIOCA (CASSAVA FLOUR)
You can get this flour toasted (torrada) or untoasted. It's used in farofa, as a thickener (in pirão) or eaten with beans.

FARINHA DE MILHO BIJU (FLAKED CORNMEAL)
Different in texture and use from the flocão de milho (see below), the biju type of cornmeal is used to make cuscuz paulista and farofa.

FARINHA DE MILHO FLOCÃO (FLAKED CORN FLOUR)
This coarse yellow cornmeal is used in cuscuz nordestino. It's similar to grits but steamed instead of boiled.

FUBÁ (FINELY GROUND CORNMEAL)
Not to be confused with polenta, it's used in classics like bolo de fubá (page 24).

MANTEIGA DE GARRAFA (BOTTLED BUTTER)

A type of clarified butter from Brazil's Northeast that's rich, slightly tangy and deeply flavourful. Substitute: Ghee.

MELADO DE CANA

A thick, dark syrup made from sugarcane juice, similar to molasses but less bitter and fruitier. Melado is used in traditional sweets, breads and even in savoury glazes.

POLVILHO AZEDO AND POLVILHO DOCE (SOUR/SWEET CASSAVA STARCH)

Used in pão de queijo and biscoito de polvilho. The sweet variety adds stretch, while the sour variety keeps food crispy. You can't substitute one for the other directly and don't confuse these with tapioca flour – they are not the same!

QUEIJO COALHO

A firm cheese that holds up well to heat and can be grilled or fried. It's used in baião de dois and served on skewers at street fairs. Substitute: Halloumi.

QUEIJO DE MANTEIGA

A slightly salty, creamy, cooked curd cheese from north-eastern Brazil, known for its melting quality and high fat content. Substitute: Gouda.

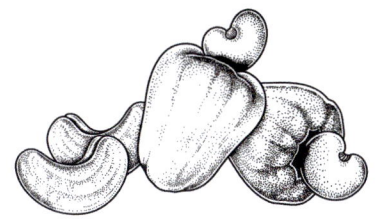

the significance of cashews

The conditions during the long sea voyage from Africa to Brazil were so harsh that many slaves died on the way or arrived severely ill. Those who were too weak were often left to die on the shores of Brazil's Northeast. Many ended up beneath cashew trees, where the fruit was often the only food they could access. After a few months, some began to recover. Much later, it was discovered that cashews are rich in vitamin C, which helped cure their symptoms, likely caused by scurvy (a disease commonly associated with sailors and travellers in the past who went without fresh fruits and vegetables for a long time).

The cashew tree is native to Brazil and was one of the many crops that spread across the world. It adapted well in India and parts of Asia. The fruit is unbelievably sweet, juicy and meaty. Its flavour is hard to pin down, but trust me, it makes a mean caipirinha (just swap the lime and thank me later). Next time you eat cashew nuts, know that every single cashew nut you've ever eaten came from its own individual fruit. Yep, one nut per fruit, just like the ones on the cover of this book.

cassava

Mandioca, macaxeira or aipim – which are all different regional names for cassava – is the root that feeds the Brazilian people. It was the basic ingredient that fed Indigenous people and later African slaves and is still present in our daily diet.

One of the most versatile ingredients on our menu, mandioca can be used in both savoury and sweet recipes. But why the different names? Botanically, mandioca brava and macaxeira/aipim are the same species. The difference lies in the variety and starch content, which leads to different culinary uses. They usually take 18 to 24 months to be ready to harvest.

Mandioca is better for making flour, polvilho and tucupi, while macaxeira/aipim is yellower and sweeter than mandioca and is best for cooking and frying. One of my mom's favourite ways of eating macaxeira was simply cooked with sugar sprinkled on top.

The word 'mandioca' comes from the Tupi-Guarani 'mani' (a mythic girl) and 'oca' (house), meaning 'the house of Mani'. This name links directly to an Indigenous legend about the origin of cassava, in which a girl named Mani dies and is buried in her home (oca), and from her grave grows the first cassava plant as a sacred gift to her people.

Cassava is used in many different ways.

① CASSAVA ROOT (MANDIOCA)
Raw cassava root, the beginning of many traditional Brazilian staples.

② PEELED CASSAVA
The thick brown skin is removed to reveal the starchy white interior.

③ GRATED CASSAVA
The cassava is finely grated, releasing its starch and juices.

④ MIXED WITH WATER AND STRAINED
Water is added and the mixture is strained to separate the liquid from the pulp. The strained cassava is then used in different ways: in tapioca and starches (polvilho); in cassava flour (farinha de mandioca); in uarini flour (farinha d'agua, or water flour); and in tucupi.

⑤ CASSAVA LEAVES (MANIÇOBA)
Even the leaves of the cassava plant are used. Nothing goes to waste.

the queen of Brazilian cuisine

Biscoito de polvilho has been a beloved snack in Brazil for centuries, originally created in the colonial era as a way use leftover polvilho (tapioca starch). The recipe was perfected in Minas Gerais and it quickly became a staple snack for tropeiros (travelling merchants), just like feijão tropeiro. Even today, it's the go-to snack for long road trips in Brazil and is sold on the beach, with vendors shouting, 'Olha o biscoito de polvilho, doce e azedo!' They can be formed into rings, and as a child I wore them on my arms like bracelets. My mom and I always favoured the sweet version. For me, this little cracker will forever taste of sun, sand and holidays.

biscoito de polvilho
tapioca crackers

SERVES 1–10*

250g (2¼ cups) polvilho azedo (sour tapioca starch)

1½ tsp salt

200ml (¾ cup + 4 tsp) hot water

2 tbsp olive oil

Preheat the oven to 200°C (400°F).

Put the polvilho azedo in a mixing bowl with the salt and any optional extras (see the tip). Add the hot water and olive oil, stirring until a smooth, uniform dough forms. The dough may feel a bit sticky at first, but let it cool slightly to make it easier to handle.

Shape the dough into small balls, long strips or rings by hand or using a piping bag. Put them directly on two baking trays – there's no need to grease or line them. Be sure to leave space between each piece, as the dough will expand while baking and the crackers may stick together if they're too close.

Bake in the preheated oven for 15–20 minutes, until crispy and lightly golden. The exact time will depend on the shape and size you chose.

Cool on wire racks before serving – the crackers will become even crunchier as they cool. Store in an airtight container for up to a month.

*This recipe may seem like it starts small, but don't be fooled – these crackers triple in size! It can serve one person or 10.

try this
Try adding a little garlic, oregano, paprika, turmeric, sesame seeds, flax seeds, Parmesan or any other spices or flavourings you like.

In Brazil, there's no such thing as life without pão de queijo. You can eat it for breakfast, lunch, dinner or as a snack. You'll always find a bag of frozen pão de queijo tucked away in a Brazilian freezer, just waiting to be baked and shared with a cuppa. Pão de queijo fresh from the oven smells like home.

The exact origin of pão de queijo remains uncertain, but it's believed to have been created in Minas Gerais in the 18th century. During that time, wheat flour was replaced with cassava flour (later known as polvilho). To avoid waste, leftover hardened cheese was mixed into the dough. Since milk and eggs were abundant, these ingredients were also incorporated, leading to the accidental creation of pão de queijo. Another theory links the recipe to the period of slavery, combining Portuguese ingredients like eggs and milk with cassava, a staple food of Indigenous Brazilians.

Pão de queijo became wildly popular after 1950, coinciding with the rise of traditional Brazilian bakeries (quitandas) that sold broas, cakes and biscuits. It spread throughout Brazil and beyond and has been beloved ever since. If you make only one recipe from this book, make this.

pão de queijo
cheese bread

MAKES 24

250g (2 cups) polvilho azedo (sour tapioca starch)

250g (2 cups) polvilho doce (sweet tapioca starch)

1 tsp salt

285ml (1 cup + 3 tbsp) milk

80ml (⅓ cup) vegetable oil

2 medium eggs

300g (3 cups) grated mature Cheddar cheese

Combine the sour tapioca starch, sweet tapioca starch and salt in a large heatproof bowl, then set aside.

Put the milk and oil in a saucepan and bring to a boil. Gradually pour the hot liquid over the starch mixture, stirring continuously. This partially cooks the starch, giving the dough its signature texture. Be careful, though, as the mixture will be hot, so stir it with a spoon so you don't burn your hands. Allow it to cool for about 10 minutes.

Add the eggs and grated Cheddar, then mix thoroughly until you have a smooth, uniform dough. If it helps, you can transfer the dough to a clean countertop and knead it with your hands just until everything comes together nicely, but don't overwork the dough or you will have heavy pão de queijo.

Roll the dough into small balls, about 50g (1¾oz) each. You should get around 24 balls.

You can bake these immediately or freeze them for later. Freezing actually enhances the flavour, but freshly baked is delicious too.

Preheat the oven to 200°C (400°F). Line two baking trays with non-stick baking paper.

- To bake them fresh, put the balls on the two lined trays. Bake in the preheated oven for 15 minutes, until golden and puffed up.
- To bake from frozen, there's no need to thaw them – just bake them straight from the freezer for 18 minutes.
- You could also cook these in an air fryer (either fresh or from frozen) at 180°C (350°F) for 15 minutes.

Pão de queijo is always best when it's warm and fresh out of the oven. If you happen to have any leftovers, store them in an airtight container for up to a week. To reheat, use a sandwich press or waffle maker to bring them back to life with a crispy outside and gooey centre.

try this

Here's a little secret: you can cut these open and add a filling. Try them with ham, a soft cheese or even a spoonful of doce de leite (dulce de leche).

My favourite dish of all! It's Bahia's axé served on a plate, a beautiful mix of ingredients and culinary influences that make this stew one of a kind. When I say axé, I mean the special energy, the good vibes, the soul, the rhythm that makes everything come alive.

bobó de camarão
shrimp stew with cassava & coconut milk

SERVES 8

600g (1lb 5oz) fresh or frozen cassava

2 x 400ml (14fl oz) tins of coconut milk

60ml (¼ cup) vegetable oil

900g (2lb) prawns, peeled and cleaned

60ml (¼ cup) azeite de dendê (red palm oil)

2 medium onions, finely chopped

1 red pepper, diced

1 green pepper, diced

1 yellow pepper, diced

2 thumb-sized pieces of ginger, peeled and grated

3 ripe tomatoes, seeds removed and diced

3 garlic cloves, minced

2 fresh red chillies, deseeded and finely chopped

1 large bunch of fresh coriander, stems and leaves separated and chopped

sea salt and freshly ground black pepper

Cut the cassava into chunks, put them in a pot and cover with water. Bring to a boil, then reduce the heat and simmer for 20–25 minutes, until very soft. Reserve a mugful of the cooking water, then drain.

Transfer the cooked cassava to a blender or food processor. Add the coconut milk and blend until smooth and creamy. If the mixture is too thick, add a bit of the reserved cassava cooking water to help it blend. Set aside.

Heat the vegetable oil in a large saucepan on a medium heat. Season the prawns with salt and pepper. Working in batches so that you don't overcrowd the pan, add the prawns to the hot oil and sear for 1 minute per side, just until lightly browned (you'll finish cooking them later). Transfer to a bowl. Cook the rest, then set aside, including any pan juices once you've cooked the last batch.

Heat the azeite de dendê in the same saucepan that you used for the prawns, still on a medium heat. Add the onions, peppers, ginger and a pinch of salt. Cook for 8 minutes, until softened. Add the diced tomatoes and cook for 4 minutes. Stir in the garlic and chillies and cook for 1 more minute.

To finish the bobó, reduce the heat and pour in the cassava cream. Stir to combine with the vegetables. Return the prawns (and any juices) to the pan and stir gently. Simmer for 2 minutes, just until the prawns are cooked through.

Turn off the heat, stir in the chopped coriander stalks (save the leaves for garnish) and adjust the salt if needed.

FOR THE PLANTAIN COCONUT FAROFA:

120g (½ cup) butter

2 plantains, sliced

1 medium onion, finely chopped

50g (½ cup) coconut flakes

300g (2¾ cups) farinha de milho biju (flaked cornmeal)

½ bunch of fresh coriander, chopped

TO SERVE:

cooked white rice

To make the plantain coconut farofa, melt the butter in a frying pan on a medium heat. When the butter starts to foam, add the sliced plantains and cook until golden on both sides. Remove from the pan and set aside on a plate.

Add the onion to the pan and cook for about 5 minutes, until translucent. Add the coconut flakes and cook for 1 minute, until they're lightly toasted. Stir in the flaked cornmeal and toast for 2–3 minutes, stirring constantly. Return the plantains to the pan, then add the chopped coriander and season with salt to taste.

Serve the bobó hot, garnished with the reserved fresh coriander leaves, with the plantain coconut farofa and cooked white rice on the side.

corn
the golden grain

Corn was part of the Indigenous diet, but it was never as dominant as cassava. The Portuguese quickly adopted it, though at first it was used to feed horses and chickens. It didn't enter the Brazilian kitchen until around 1618, when it began appearing in cakes and other sweet preparations. Portuguese women worked wonders with corn. Combined with milk, eggs and sugar, new dishes were born. Africans also made great use of corn, adding it to dishes like mungunzá (a sweet corn porridge) and angú (like a Brazilian version of polenta).

Across the rest of the American continent and the Amerindian islands, corn was a symbol of sustenance and identity. The Aztecs, Incas and Mayans relied heavily on it for nourishment.

It's said that corn travelled from north to south, while cassava moved in the opposite direction. As cassava made its way north, it became known as yuca. There's an ongoing debate about the exact journey of corn through the Americas, but most researchers agree it was first domesticated around 9,000 years ago in southern Mexico from a wild grass called teosinte.

But one thing is certain: corn spread across the world like no other ingredient. In Brazil, it became the heart of many traditional dishes and gave rise to staples like fubá, flocão de milho, biju de milho, canjiquinha and canjica.

Corn is celebrated throughout the month of June. It's planted in January and harvested in June, just in time for São João, a beloved festival where countless treats are made from corn.

This was one of my mom's signature dishes. You know the kind of recipe you share with friends and they always come back saying, 'I made it, but it just didn't taste the same as yours'? In Brazil, we say 'não tem a sua mão' ('it doesn't have your touch'). And my mom really did have that magic touch.

Couscous is a traditional dish from North Africa, made with semolina. When the Portuguese arrived in Brazil, they already knew couscous from places like Morocco and Tunisia, but since semolina wasn't available, they swapped it for cornmeal. This São Paulo version is a hearty mix of cornmeal, vegetables, tomato sauce and sardines, all cooked in a pot and then turned out in a Bundt tin for serving. My mom always used tuna instead of sardines, which I think is even tastier.

cuscuz paulista
savoury cornmeal cake

SERVES 6

1 egg
1 green pepper
1 red pepper
1 yellow pepper
4 tsp vegetable oil, plus extra for greasing
1 medium onion, finely chopped
3 x 145g (5oz) tins of tuna in oil, about half of the oil reserved
1 x 200g (7oz) tin of sweetcorn
500g (2 cups) good-quality shop-bought tomato sauce
a handful of fresh flat-leaf parsley, chopped, plus a few large leaves to garnish
a handful of fresh chives, chopped
130g (1 cup) farinha de milho biju (flaked cornmeal)
a few pitted black olives, sliced
sea salt and freshly ground black pepper

Put the egg in a saucepan, cover it with cold water and bring to a boil, then reduce the heat and simmer for 10 minutes. Transfer the egg to a bowl of ice water to stop it cooking. When it's cool enough to handle, peel it and cut into slices.

Meanwhile, dice about one-quarter of each pepper. (Save the rest for the pulled banana peels on page 42.)

Heat the oil in a large saucepan on a medium heat. Add the diced peppers and onion and cook for 8–10 minutes, until soft. Stir in the tuna and about half of the oil from the tins. Add the sweetcorn, tomato sauce and chopped fresh herbs and stir to combine. Season to taste with salt and pepper, then cook for 5 minutes. Gradually add the flaked cornmeal, stirring constantly to prevent lumps. Cook for a few minutes, until the mixture thickens and holds together.

Lightly grease a medium-sized Bundt cake tin (a plain Bundt tin works best for this rather than a more decorative one). Line the bottom with slices of hard-boiled egg, whole parsley leaves and sliced olives. Spoon the couscous mixture into the mould, pressing it down gently.

Let it cool and firm up for 15 minutes, then unmould onto a serving plate. Serve warm or at room temperature.

As the name 'nordestino' implies, this dish is from Brazil's Northeast. I first tried cuscuz nordestino when I was an adult; it wasn't as popular when I was growing up as it is today. It's the king of breakfast, but it's just as good for lunch or dinner, in both savoury and sweet versions. The way it's prepared is quite different from the cuscuz paulista on the previous page, and it even uses a different type of corn flour. What I love most is its versatility.

cuscuz nordestino
steamed corn couscous

SERVES 2

100g (1 cup) farinha de milho flocão (flaked corn flour)

½ tsp salt

80ml (⅓ cup) water

50g (1¾oz) cheese (such as queijo coalho, mozzarella or Cheddar), cut into small cubes

a knob of butter

Put the flaked corn flour and salt in a bowl and stir together. Gradually drizzle in the water while stirring with a spoon to moisten the flour evenly. The texture should resemble wet sand: soft and crumbly, but moist. Let it sit for 10 minutes to hydrate so the flakes soften before steaming.

Fill the bottom of a cuscuzeira (Brazilian couscous steamer) with water and fit the steamer basket into place. Transfer half of the hydrated corn mixture into the basket without pressing it down. Spread the cheese cubes evenly in the centre, then cover with the remaining corn mixture. Again, don't pack it down – keeping it loose allows the steam to pass through and cook it evenly.

Cover the steamer with the lid and put it on a high heat on the hob. Once the water begins to boil, you'll notice a light steam escaping from the sides of the lid. Lower the heat and cook for about 10 minutes, until the couscous is fluffy and tender.

Turn off the heat. Carefully remove the basket (watch out for steam!) and gently pull the central stem to release the couscous from the mould.

If you don't have a cuscuzeira, put half of the hydrated flaked corn flour in the middle of a clean cotton cloth, then spread the cheese cubes evenly across the top. Cover with the rest of the corn flour, then tie the cloth closed. Put the cloth in a sieve, then put the sieve on a pot filled about one-quarter full of water (you don't want the water to touch the bottom of the sieve). Cover the sieve with a lid, then bring to a boil and steam.

Transfer to a plate. Serve warm with the butter on top to let it melt gently over the couscous and enjoy the surprise of the melting cheese inside.

5 ways to enjoy

1 WITH BUTTER (CUSCUZ COM MANTEIGA): The simplest and most traditional way – steamed couscous is served hot and topped with butter, which melts into the soft cornmeal.

2 WITH CHEESE (CUSCUZ COM QUEIJO): Slices of coalho cheese (a firm, slightly salty Brazilian cheese, similar to halloumi) are added to the couscous while it steams, creating a melty texture.

3 WITH EGGS (CUSCUZ COM OVO): Served alongside fried or scrambled eggs, sometimes with a bit of carne de sol (sun-dried beef) for extra protein.

4 WITH MEAT OR CHICKEN: Couscous is also enjoyed with shredded chicken, carne de sol or ground beef, making it a heartier meal.

5 SWEET VERSION: For a sweet twist, some people mix couscous with sugar, coconut milk and grated coconut, turning it into a simple, comforting dessert.

'Fica que vai ter bolo!' ('Stay, we're having cake!') Add a simple 'Eu vou passar um café' ('I'll make some coffee') and you know what that means: a long afternoon full of gossip. And if the cake on the table is cornmeal cake with guava sauce, that's guaranteed to be the best kind of gossip. Cake with coffee is pure grandma's house vibes, and I don't just mean my grandma. Ask any Brazilian and they'll say the same thing.

In Brazil, our love for corn-based treats comes from the Indigenous people, while the word 'fubá' itself comes from Kimbundu, an African language, where it means 'flour'. This cornmeal cake was born in colonial times as a more affordable alternative to the fancy cakes made with expensive wheat flour imported from Portugal. Over time, the Portuguese helped spread corn-based baking across the country and fubá became a staple in Brazilian kitchens.

bolo de fubá com calda de goiabada
cornmeal cake with guava sauce
SERVES 10–12

melted butter, for greasing

150g (1¼ cups) fubá (finely ground cornmeal)

200ml (¾ cup + 4 tsp) hot milk

2 eggs

150g (¾ cup) caster sugar

60g (½ cup) grated mozzarella cheese

120ml (½ cup) vegetable oil, plus extra for greasing

1 tbsp baking powder

½ tsp salt

FOR THE GUAVA SAUCE:

150g (⅔ cup) guava paste

160ml (⅔ cup) water

Preheat the oven to 180°C (350°F). Grease a Bundt tin with melted butter and oil using a pastry brush. You won't need to dust the tin with flour, and the result will be a clean release and a much neater-looking cake.

Put the cornmeal and hot milk in a mixing bowl. Stir to combine, then let it rest for 10 minutes to hydrate the cornmeal. Transfer to a blender or food processor, then add the eggs, sugar, cheese, oil, baking powder and salt. Blend until smooth.

Pour the batter into the greased Bundt tin. Bake in the preheated oven for 30 minutes, until a skewer inserted into the centre of the cake comes out clean. Let the cake cool slightly before turning it upside down and removing it from the tin.

Meanwhile, to make the guava sauce, put the guava paste and water in a small saucepan on a low heat. Stir constantly until the paste melts and forms a smooth sauce (or you can do this in a microwave).

Drizzle the warm guava sauce over the cake before cutting into slices to serve.

If you like custard, you'll love curau. This was a dish I always ate at a place called Rancho da Pamonha, a roadside restaurant that served only corn-based dishes, and curau was my go-to. We'd stop there on Sunday afternoons after the visits to my grandmothers' houses.

This traditional Brazilian corn dessert has its origins in European puddings and a thick beverage used by the Tupi Indigenous people. In fact, the word 'curau' comes from the Tupi term 'minga'u', which refers to a dense, corn-based drink that's also used in rituals.

curau de milho
sweetcorn custard

SERVES 4

600g (1lb 5oz) fresh corn kernels (weight after cutting off the cob)

500ml (2 cups) milk

120g (½ heaped cup) caster sugar

a pinch of ground cinnamon

try this
Don't discard the leftover corn pulp! You can mix it into your granola or toast it for a crunchy topping on salads.

Cut the corn kernels from the cobs, then put the kernels in a blender with the milk and blitz until smooth. Pass the blended mixture through a fine mesh sieve or cheesecloth to extract as much liquid as possible, leaving behind any solids (see the tip).

Pour the strained liquid into a saucepan and stir in the sugar. Cook on a medium heat, stirring constantly, for 20–25 minutes, until the mixture thickens.

Divide the custard among four ramekins or serving bowls. Refrigerate until set – it should be firm but creamy. Just before serving, sprinkle a little ground cinnamon over the top of each one.

> **This was a dish I always ate at a place called Rancho da Pamonha, a roadside restaurant that served only corn-based dishes, and curau was my go-to. We'd stop there on Sunday afternoons after the visits to my grandmothers' houses.**

Archaeological evidence suggests that beans were being grown and consumed in Latin America over 7,000 years ago. Beans were a staple food for ancient civilisations such as the Aztecs, Mayans and Incas, who cultivated several different species.

In Brazil, Indigenous peoples were consuming beans long before the arrival of European colonisers. By the second half of the 16th century, beans (both in pods and dried) were already being traded in the markets of Salvador, Bahia. Indigenous peoples were the primary food suppliers to the new settlers, offering a wide variety of crops from their traditional gardens, including beans, corn, pumpkin and cassava. They practised intercropping, including planting beans with corn, a method that naturally enriches the soil thanks to the bean plant's ability to fix nitrogen in the soil. This mutual relationship also benefits the climbing bean plants, which use the corn stalks for support.

a Brazilian staple

The beans consumed by Indigenous Brazilians belonged to the *Phaseolus* genus and were traditionally cooked in clay pots. These exchanges between Indigenous peoples and the Portuguese were foundational in shaping early Brazilian agriculture and cuisine.

While beans were already part of the Indigenous diet long before colonisation, rice was introduced to Brazil by the Portuguese, who brought varieties from Asia and Africa during the colonial period. Despite their different origins, rice and beans eventually came together to form one of the most iconic elements of the Brazilian plate. Their association has played, and continues to play, a vital role in Brazilian culture and agriculture. However, this culinary union was not instantaneous. It took time for rice and beans to become a daily staple in Brazil's main meal of the day. Over time, these two ingredients have become inseparable on the Brazilian table.

black bean stew

Ask any Brazilian how feijoada was created, and they'll likely tell you that it was created by Brazilian slaves, who supposedly made the dish using the scraps of pork discarded by their owners. However, this theory has some flaws. For starters, during that time, cuts like the pig's head, tail and feet were considered delicacies and were unlikely to have been thrown away.

Feijoada evolved from Portuguese cuisine, specifically a pork and vegetable stew from the Minho province in northern Portugal. This type of dish wasn't unique to Brazil – similar stews were common across Europe in the 16th to 18th centuries, a time marked by food scarcity. Well-known European examples include French cassoulet, Spanish cocido madrileño and Italian fagiolata.

Like many other colonial-era dishes, feijoada was adapted in Brazil with local ingredients, like black beans, which were native to the region. Of course, we gave it our own flair, seasoning and soul, and that's what made it the beloved dish it is today. But its origins? Firmly Portuguese.

Today, feijoada is more than a meal – it's a tradition. In São Paulo, restaurants typically serve it on Wednesdays and Saturdays, a practice inherited from Portuguese settlers who associated specific dishes with certain weekdays. Think of it as 'Taco Tuesday', but for feijoada!

feijoada
black bean stew

SERVES 10

1kg (2¼lb) carne seca (Brazilian dried beef, or substitute with salted beef)

1kg (5 cups) dried black beans

1 x 680g (1½lb) smoked pork rib rack

200g (7oz) pork belly

3 linguiças calabresa (Brazilian smoked sausages, or substitute with chorizo or kielbasa)

1 orange, unpeeled and quartered

8 bay leaves

2 onions, roughly chopped

5 spring onions

4 garlic cloves

½ bunch of fresh flat-leaf parsley

TRADITIONAL SIDES:

banana frita

farofa

couve

boiled white rice

vinaigrette (salsa)

orange slices

torresmo (crispy pork cracklings)

Rinse the carne seca under cold running water, then soak it in cold water for at least 12 hours, changing the water every 3–4 hours. This method is ideal for carne seca imported from Brazil. If using carne seca produced elsewhere, simply cut it into large cubes and add it directly to the pot, no soaking required.

Put the black beans in a colander and rinse under cold running water, then transfer to a large pot. Drain the carne seca and cut it into large chunks, then add it to the pot along with the rack of ribs, pork belly and sausages, leaving them all whole – they will be cut into smaller pieces after cooking.

Fill the pot with enough water to completely cover the beans and meats. Add the orange and bay leaves, then bring to a boil. Reduce the heat and simmer, uncovered, for 2 hours, stirring occasionally.

Remove the meats from the pot as they become tender, in this order: pork ribs, pork belly, sausages, dried beef. Cut the meats into small pieces. Discard the orange and bay leaves.

Put the onions, spring onions, garlic and parsley in a blender with a bit of the feijoada cooking liquid to help it all blend. Blitz until smooth, then pour this mixture back into the pot, stirring to combine. Let it cook for another hour.

Return the meats to the feijoada. Taste and adjust the salt.

I always prepare the feijoada one day in advance because the flavour deepens and improves overnight, but cook the traditional sides (banana frita, farofa, couve, rice and vinaigrette) on the day of serving. Reheat the feijoada and serve everything together as a feast, with orange slices and crispy pork crackling as garnish.

banana frita
fried banana

Peel **5 firm, ripe (but not overly soft) bananas** and cut each one into three pieces. (The amounts here serve 10 for a feijoada feast, but you can scale it down – allow half a banana per person.)

Set up your breading station with three wide, shallow bowls: first **80g (⅔ cup) plain flour**, then **2 beaten eggs**, then **100g (1 cup) dried or panko breadcrumbs**. Lightly dust each banana piece with flour, then dip into the beaten eggs, ensuring it's fully coated. Finally, roll it in the breadcrumbs, pressing gently to adhere.

Heat **500ml (2 cups) sunflower oil** in a high-sided frying pan or saucepan on a medium heat. Working in batches so that you don't overcrowd the pan, add the breaded bananas and fry for 2–3 minutes, until golden brown on both sides. Drain on a plate lined with kitchen paper to remove any excess oil. Enjoy as a side for feijoada or as a sweet treat with sugar and cinnamon sprinkled on top.

farofa

I could happily eat farofa at every meal. Sometimes I wonder if it's in my son's DNA, because when I was pregnant, one of my cravings was farofa. I once ate an entire plate of it and landed in the hospital, but that's a story for another day.

To call farofa a staple in Brazilian cuisine is an understatement. It's essential. Made traditionally with cassava flour (either plain or toasted), farofa has an irresistible crunch and nutty aroma that makes a plate feel complete (just don't eat a full plate of it!).

Cook **150g (5oz) diced bacon** in a hot, dry pan on a medium heat until it's crispy. Add **1 large finely chopped onion** to the fat that's rendered out of the bacon and cook for 5–8 minutes, until soft. Add **150g (⅔ cup) diced butter** and let it fully melt. Crack **2 eggs** directly into the pan and stir to scramble. Gradually add **180g (1½ cups) farinha de mandioca torrada (toasted cassava flour) or ready-made farofa flour**, stirring well to coat it with the butter and to let it absorb the flavours. Mix in **80g (⅔ cup) pitted, sliced black olives**, **5 thinly sliced spring onions** and ½ **bunch of chopped fresh flat-leaf parsley**, then adjust the **salt** to taste. Serve warm as a side for feijoada, grilled meats or Brazilian barbecue.

couve
sautéed collard greens

Collard greens are the best choice here, but York cabbage works perfectly and can be easier to find. Heat **a splash of olive oil** in a large frying pan on a medium heat. Add **1.5kg (3¼lb) collard greens or** ½ **head of thinly sliced York cabbage** and **4 thinly sliced garlic cloves** and cook for 30 seconds, just until the greens have lightly wilted. Season with **salt**. Transfer to a serving platter and serve hot.

Feijão tropeiro was a staple meal for the tropeiros (travelling merchants, drovers and muleteers) who spent weeks on the road transporting goods like gold, coffee and livestock across Brazil during the 17th to 19th centuries. They also played a key role in spreading news, culture and even revolutionary ideas throughout the country. Some historians believe that tropeiros helped circulate messages supporting Brazil's independence from Portugal as they travelled between major economic hubs like São Paulo, Minas Gerais and Goiás. The ingredients in feijão tropeiro – beans, dried meat, cassava flour and cured sausage – were all long-lasting and easy to carry, making this dish the perfect trail food.

feijão tropeiro
cattle drovers' beans

SERVES 4

120g (½ cup) dried feijão carioca (pinto beans) (about 300g (1¾ cups) cooked)

2–3 bay leaves

2 tbsp vegetable oil

150g (5¼oz) bacon, diced

300g (10½oz) cabanossi sausage, cut into large cubes

1 medium onion, chopped

2 garlic cloves, minced

1 fresh red chilli, deseeded and finely chopped

85g (3oz) collard greens or kale, thinly sliced

4 eggs

90g (6 tbsp) butter or lard

100g (¾ cup) farinha de mandioca (cassava flour) or farinha de milho biju (flaked cornmeal)

60g (2oz) cherry tomatoes, quartered

4 spring onions

½ bunch of fresh flat-leaf parsley

sea salt and freshly ground black pepper

If using dried beans, soak them in cold water for at least 6 hours or overnight. Drain, then transfer to a pot and cover with plenty of fresh cold water. There's no need to season at this stage, but for truly Brazilian beans, add 2–3 bay leaves. Bring to a boil, then reduce the heat and simmer, uncovered, for 45–60 minutes, until soft (or for 15–20 minutes in a pressure cooker). Drain and discard the bay leaves.

Heat the oil in a large frying pan on a medium heat. Add the bacon and cook until it's crispy, then add the sausage and cook for a few minutes. Add the onion, garlic and chilli and cook for 5–8 minutes, until the onion is soft.

Add the sliced collard greens or kale and cook just until lightly wilted. Crack the eggs directly into the pan, stirring and scrambling them until fully cooked. Gently stir in the cooked beans, mixing carefully to avoid mashing them.

Add the butter or lard and let it melt completely before gradually adding the cassava flour, stirring until everything is well incorporated. Season with salt and pepper, then finish with the cherry tomatoes, spring onions and parsley scattered on top.

Serve warm with boiled rice, with hot sauce on the side if desired. This dish is complete on its own, but you can also serve it with a fried egg and/or torresmo (pork crackling) on top, or as a side at a barbecue.

TO SERVE:
boiled white rice
hot sauce (optional)
fried egg
torresmo (pork cracklings)

Baião de dois is both a dish and the name of a song. Baião is a traditional folk rhythm and dance from Ceará, popularised by Humberto Teixeira and Luiz Gonzaga; their 'Baião de Dois' helped cement the name. The dish – black-eyed peas and rice cooked together – looks like a couple dancing, moving as one. It was born in lean times when nothing could go to waste: rice, beans and whatever was left in the kitchen, brought together out of necessity and turned into comfort.

baião de dois
rice & beans with meat & cheese

SERVES 8

1kg (2¼lb) carne seca (Brazilian dried beef)

250g (1½ cups) dried feijão fradinho (black-eyed peas) or 2 x 400g (14oz) tins, drained and rinsed

2–3 bay leaves

300g (10½oz) bacon, diced

300g (10½oz) linguiças calabresa (Brazilian smoked sausages, or substitute with chorizo or kielbasa), diced

1 large onion, chopped

4 ripe tomatoes, diced

4 garlic cloves, finely chopped

1 small fresh red chilli, finely chopped

250g (1⅓ cups) basmati rice

50g (2oz) manteiga de garrafa (Brazilian bottled butter) or ghee

300g (10½oz) halloumi cheese, diced (a close substitute for Brazilian queijo coalho)

4 spring onions, thinly sliced

1 bunch of fresh coriander, chopped

sea salt and freshly ground black pepper

Rinse the carne seca under cold running water, then soak it in cold water for at least 12 hours, changing the water every 3–4 hours. This method is ideal for carne seca imported from Brazil. If using carne seca produced elsewhere, skip the soaking – simply cut it into large cubes and proceed straight to cooking.

If using dried beans, soak them in cold water for at least 6 hours or overnight. Drain, then transfer the beans to a pot and cover with fresh cold water. There's no need to season at this stage, but for truly Brazilian beans, add 2–3 bay leaves. Bring to a boil, then reduce the heat and simmer, uncovered, for 45–60 minutes, until soft (or cook for 15–20 minutes in a pressure cooker). Drain and discard the bay leaves.

Boil the carne seca in a large saucepan of fresh water for about 2 hours, until tender (or for 40 minutes in a pressure cooker). Once cooked, reserve the cooking water, then shred the meat, removing any excess fat.

Put a large frying pan on a medium heat. Add the bacon and cook until crispy – its fat will render out, so no extra oil is needed at this stage. Add the sausage and cook until it's nicely browned all over. Add the onion, tomatoes, garlic and chilli and cook for 8–10 minutes, until everything is soft and fragrant.

Add the rice to the pan and stir well to coat. Pour in just enough of the reserved cooking liquid to cover the rice.

TO SERVE (OPTIONAL):
torresmo (pork cracklings)
fried eggs (one per person)
fried bananas (page 33)

Cook until all the liquid has been absorbed into the rice, which will still be undercooked. This is the perfect moment to add the cooked beans, the shredded beef and enough additional cooking liquid to cover the mixture. Let everything cook together for 15–20 minutes, until the rice and beans are fully tender.

Meanwhile, melt the manteiga de garrafa or ghee in a separate frying pan on a medium heat, then add the diced halloumi. Cook for a couple of minutes, until lightly golden brown on both sides, then set aside.

Once the rice and beans are fully cooked, stir in the browned halloumi along with the spring onions and fresh coriander. Give everything a quick stir to combine and season to taste.

Serve hot just as it is or with torresmo (pork cracklings), one fried egg per person and fried bananas (page 33). I love all three, but you will need to lie down and have a nap afterwards!

banana

Brazil's beloved fruit

Bananas are the most popular fruit in Brazil. They're easy to eat, fill you up and please every palate. They can be fried, boiled or baked. They bring joy, both culturally and nutritionally – their natural sugars and nutrients are gentle mood boosters. Could that be the secret to the Brazilian spirit?

Even though bananas are a beloved fruit, they aren't native to Brazil. Historical records show that bananas were brought to the Americas from the Canary Islands around 1516. Originally from Southeast Asia, bananas travelled through Africa before reaching Brazil, where they were quickly naturalised. In some regions, particularly in the Amazon and the Northeast, bananas were known by their Tupi name, pacova, a name used to describe banana da terra, or plantain.

Bananas are serious business in Brazil. We're one of the largest producers in the world, and the fruit is part of daily life across the country. At the market, you'll typically find five main types, each with its own flavour, texture and use.

❶ **BANANA NANICA (SHORT BANANA):** The most common type. Despite the name ('nanica' means short), the plant is tall. With its sweet, soft flesh, it's the most widely consumed type of banana in Brazil and is often exported.

❷ **BANANA PRATA (SILVER BANANA):** Small to medium-sized with a firm texture, long shelf life and slightly acidic flavour.

❸ **BANANA OURO (GOLDEN BANANA):** Tiny, intensely sweet and golden-skinned, this type is considered a delicacy and is often eaten fresh.

❹ **BANANA MAÇÃ (BANANA APPLE):** Smaller and sweet, with a hint of apple aroma, banana maçã is very fragrant but bruises easily.

❺ **BANANA DA TERRA (PLANTAIN):** Large, firm and starchy, plantains are usually cooked, fried, boiled or baked and are often used in savoury dishes.

This is a special recipe from my mom. She used to save all the old bread in a pan inside the oven, letting it dry out until the pan was full. Then she would toast the pieces, grind them into breadcrumbs and portion them into bags for storing in the freezer. One of her favourite ways to use those breadcrumbs was in this quick, one-bowl banana bread. The recipe doesn't need any flour because it makes brilliant use of one of the most wasted ingredients in our homes.

bolo de banana
banana bread

MAKES 1 LOAF

450g (1lb) bananas (about 4), peeled

300g (1¾ cups) dark brown sugar

2 eggs

120ml (½ cup) vegetable oil

250g (2½ cups) fresh breadcrumbs

1 tbsp baking powder

a pinch of ground cinnamon (optional)

Preheat the oven to 180°C (350°F). Grease and line a 900g (2lb) loaf tin.

Put the peeled bananas in a large bowl and mash with a fork until smooth. Add the sugar, eggs and oil, mixing well. Add the breadcrumbs, stirring until fully combined, then stir in the baking powder and cinnamon (if using).

Pour the batter into the prepared loaf tin. Bake in the preheated oven for 45 minutes, until a skewer inserted into the centre comes out clean.

Allow to cool on a wire rack before cutting into slices.

top tip
Save the peels to make the carne louca de casca de banana (pulled banana peels) on the next page.

This was my mother's wooden spoon. It has travelled thousands of miles from her kitchen to mine.

This recipe is a fresh take on Brazil's beloved carne louca (braised beef sandwich), a classic party dish often served in pão francês (which is a typical Brazilian bread, despite the French name) at birthday celebrations. By using the banana peel that's commonly discarded, this recipe is transforming a waste product into a tasty and sustainable twist on a favourite Brazilian street food.

carne louca de casca de banana
pulled banana peels

SERVES 4

peels from 6 bananas
60ml (¼ cup) olive oil
1 medium onion, sliced
¼ red pepper, sliced
¼ green pepper, sliced
¼ yellow pepper, sliced
250g (1 cup) good-quality ready-made tomato sauce
100g (⅔ cup) pitted green olives, roughly chopped
a pinch of paprika
4 spring onions, chopped
¼ bunch of fresh flat-leaf parsley, chopped
sea salt and freshly ground black pepper

TO SERVE:
sandwich rolls, tortillas or boiled white rice

Save your banana peels and store them in the fridge until you have six peels and are ready to use them. With a spoon, scrape off the soft white flesh from the inside of each peel. Slice the peels very thinly with a sharp knife.

Heat the oil in a large frying pan on a medium heat. Add the onion and peppers and cook for 5–7 minutes, until softened. Stir in the shredded banana peels, tomato sauce, green olives, paprika and salt and pepper to taste. Cook for 10–15 minutes, stirring occasionally, until the flavours are well blended and the peels are tender. Turn off the heat and stir in the chopped spring onions and parsley.

Serve warm on sandwich rolls, tucked into tortillas for tacos or spooned over boiled white rice.

The fusion of techniques and spices from Portuguese, African and Indigenous cultures helped make this dessert one of the most famous in Pernambuco. Its origins trace back to the old sugarcane mills. Because it carries influences from the three main peoples that shape the country's culture, cartola is considered a truly Brazilian dessert.

cartola
banana with cheese

SERVES 1

2 tbsp manteiga de garrafa (Brazilian bottled butter) or ghee

1 banana, cut in half lengthways

85g (3oz) queijo manteiga (a buttery Brazilian cheese) or a mild, melty cheese like mozzarella, Monterey Jack or Gouda, sliced

a pinch of ground cinnamon

a pinch of caster sugar

a drizzle of melado de cana (sugarcane syrup) or molasses

Warm the manteiga de garrafa or ghee in a small frying pan on a medium heat. Add the banana and fry until golden brown on both sides. Remove from the pan and set aside on a serving plate.

Add the cheese to the pan and cook until golden and slightly melted, flipping once.

Put the cheese on top of the banana. Sprinkle with cinnamon and sugar, then drizzle with melado de cana or molasses and serve while it's still warm.

manteiga de garrafa
a taste of Brazil's Northeast

Manteiga de garrafa, also known as butter oil or ghee from Brazil, is a type of clarified butter traditionally used in Northeastern Brazilian cuisine. Unlike regular butter, it's liquid at room temperature due to its high level of clarified milk fat and lack of water content. Its rich, nutty flavour and golden colour make it a staple in dishes like cartola, baião de dois (page 36) and paçoca de carne seca (page 58). Historically, this butter was developed to preserve dairy in hot climates before refrigeration was common. By removing the milk solids and water, the butter lasts longer and can be stored without refrigeration, making it ideal for cooking in tropical conditions. It's commonly sold in bottles, hence the name 'manteiga de garrafa' ('bottled butter').

sweet and savoury versatility

It's hard to imagine Brazilian cuisine without coconut, but the coconut didn't exist in Brazil at the time of its 'discovery' by the Portuguese in 1500. The first references appear in the Descriptive Treaty of Brazil, written by Gabriel Soares de Sousa in 1587, where he states, 'The palm trees that bear coconuts thrive in Bahia, even more so than in India, because planting a coconut in the ground yields a palm that produces fruit in five to six years, whereas in India, these plants do not bear fruit for 20 years.'

The giant coconut palm was first introduced to Brazil in 1553, in the state of Bahia. It came from the Cape Verde islands but its distant origin is believed to be India or Sri Lanka, from where coconuts were introduced to Mozambique.

From Bahia, the coconut palm spread along the northeastern coast of Brazil, where it found favourable conditions for cultivation because it's a fruit tree typical of tropical climates. Over time, it eventually adapted to other regions of the country. Today, coconut palms are grown in almost every state across Brazil.

Coconut started being used in cooking by the people who lived by the sea. In Bahia, coastal cooking really embraces coconut, using both the flesh and the milk to add flavour to dishes. The expansion to other regions happened when coastal families moved inland and brought their food habits with them.

Coconut eventually became an essential ingredient in Brazil's Northeast. It shows up in recipes for breakfast, lunch, dinner and dessert. It may not be native, but it's become a signature Brazilian ingredient.

Moqueca is a dish that beautifully expresses the blend of cultures that shaped Brazil. Its origins trace back to Indigenous peoples, who wrapped fish in leaves – a method known as pokeka, from the Tupi word meaning 'wrapped'. These fish were often slow-cooked over rustic grills called moquém, which inspired the name 'moqueca'. When the Portuguese arrived, they brought their tradition of hearty stews (cozidos) with them, which merged with native ingredients and tropical fish. Later, African influences added depth and boldness, introducing dendê oil, coconut milk and chillies, especially in Bahia. Today, moqueca remains one of Brazil's most cherished recipes, with the handcrafted clay pot as its signature element, no matter the version or region.

And then there's pirão, the beloved sidekick: a thick, comforting gravy made from fish broth and cassava flour, stirred until smooth and creamy, that rounds out the dish with its earthy texture and deep flavour. Like moqueca, pirão has strong Indigenous roots.

moqueca de peixe com pirão
Brazilian fish stew

SERVES 4

1 x 400ml (14fl oz) tin of coconut milk

4 tsp dendê oil (red palm oil)

½ tsp sea salt, plus extra to season

900g (2lb) haddock fillets, skinned

1 tbsp olive oil

1 medium onion, sliced

3 garlic cloves, finely chopped

1 fresh red chilli, finely chopped

2 medium tomatoes, sliced

½ yellow pepper, sliced

½ green pepper, sliced

½ bunch of fresh coriander, leaves and stems chopped, plus extra leaves to garnish

Put the coconut milk, dendê oil and salt in a blender and blitz for 1 minute, until fully emulsified. Set aside.

Lightly season the haddock fillets with salt on both sides. Set aside while you prepare the vegetables.

Heat the olive oil in a medium saucepan or deep frying pan (or for a true Brazilian experience, a black clay pot) on a medium heat. Add the onion, garlic, chilli and a pinch of salt. Cook for about 2 minutes, until the onion starts to soften. Add the sliced tomatoes and peppers in an even layer, then put the seasoned fish fillets on top. Pour over the coconut milk mixture – the fish should be partially submerged. The fish will release water, so don't be tempted to add more liquid.

Cover the pan with a lid and simmer gently for 10 minutes, until the fish is cooked through but still moist and the vegetables are tender.

Meanwhile, to make the pirão, heat the dendê oil in a large saucepan on a medium heat. Add the red pepper, tomato, onion and garlic and cook for 5–8 minutes, until soft. Add the fish stock and bring to a boil.

yellow rice

To make yellow rice, just add a pinch of turmeric to the water you cook your rice in.

FOR THE PIRÃO:

1 tsp dendê oil (red palm oil)

¼ red pepper, roughly chopped

1 tomato, roughly chopped

1 small onion, roughly chopped

1 garlic clove, chopped

250ml (1 cup) fish stock

50g (⅓ heaped cup) farinha de mandioca (cassava flour) (adjust for desired thickness)

TO SERVE:

yellow rice (see the note)

Blitz using a hand blender until smooth (be careful since the liquid is hot). Bring back to a simmer, then gradually whisk in the cassava flour until you reach your desired consistency – thicker for a hearty pirão or lighter for a saucier version.

To finish, stir the chopped fresh coriander into the stew, then add extra whole leaves on top to garnish.

Serve hot with the pirão and yellow rice on the side.

Although I'm making this as an individual dessert, my mom always made the big family version called quindão (same recipe, just baked in a big Bundt tin). Hers had way more coconut, of course. The real challenge with quindim is making sure it doesn't taste too eggy, but if you follow my instructions, I promise yours won't.

Quindim is a traditional Brazilian dessert that originated as an adaptation of Portuguese convent sweets, which were originally made with almond flour. Due to the scarcity of almonds in Brazil, coconut was used instead, giving quindim its signature tropical flavour. The dessert's name comes from Bantu languages, brought by African influences, and means 'something sweet or charming'. Traditionally baked in small ramekins, quindim is a beloved treat and is often served at celebrations.

quindim
coconut custard

MAKES 9

10 egg yolks

275g (1⅓ cups) caster sugar, plus extra for dusting

100g (1¼ cups) fresh or frozen grated coconut

45g (3 tbsp) unsalted butter, melted and cooled, plus extra for greasing

Grease nine mini pudding moulds with butter and dust them with sugar to prevent sticking. Set aside.

Strain the egg yolks into a mixing bowl through a fine mesh sieve. You want to prevent the thin skin on the yolks from passing through. Add the sugar, coconut and melted butter, mixing until well combined. Let the batter rest for 15–20 minutes to allow the coconut to absorb the liquid and enhance the texture.

Preheat the oven to 180°C (350°F).

Pour the mixture into the prepared moulds. Put the moulds in a roasting tin, then pour in enough hot water to come halfway up the sides of the moulds to create a bain-marie (water bath) to cook the custards gently and evenly.

Bake in the preheated oven for 45–50 minutes, until the tops are firm and slightly golden. Let the quindims cool before running a knife around the edges to release them.

To serve, carefully invert each one onto a plate to reveal the glossy, golden tops.

Cocada is a simple mix of grated coconut, sugar and water, but this version with condensed milk is my favourite. It makes the centre extra moist and gooey, the kind of bite that melts in your mouth and keeps you going back for just one more piece.

cocada
coconut sweets

MAKES 16

240g (1¼ cups) caster sugar

300ml (1¼ cups) water

300g (3¾ cups) fresh or frozen grated coconut

1 x 400ml (14fl oz) tin of sweetened condensed milk

Put the sugar and water in a saucepan and cook on a medium heat until it reaches a thin thread consistency (when a small amount of syrup drips from a spoon in a thin, steady thread), which is 106°C–107°C (223°F–225°F) on a candy thermometer.

Remove the pan from the heat and add the grated coconut, mixing well to incorporate. Immediately add the sweetened condensed milk and return the pan to the heat. Stir continuously for 20–25 minutes, until the mixture thickens and starts to pull away from the bottom of the pan or until you see that all the liquid has evaporated, the mixture feels consistent and it's not sticking to the bottom of the pan.

Remove the pan from the heat. Wait 1 minute, until the mixture settles. Using two spoons, shape the mixture into small quenelles or oval scoops. Put them on a piece of parchment paper and let them cool and dry for about 1 hour before serving. Store any leftovers in an airtight container at room temperature for up to a week.

carne seca

Brazilian dried beef

Carne seca, charque, jabá, carne velha, carne do ceará and carne de sol are just a few of the many names Brazilians use for dried meat. While they all fall under the same broad category, there are subtle differences between them.

The earliest historical records of carne seca date back to the early 17th century in Brazil's Northeast. The technique of salting and drying beef has deep historical roots linked to Portuguese colonisers, who brought with them drying and salting skills to make products like salted cod (bacalhau). The early ranchers and cowboys in Brazil's Northeast simply adapted the Portuguese salt-curing techniques for beef, creating the first Brazilian carne seca.

Its creation was driven by necessity, both to preserve the large quantities of meat being produced at the time and to solve the challenges of transporting food across long distances in a hot, humid climate. Over time, carne seca became part of the cultural identity of the Sertanejo people. It symbolised resilience, resourcefulness and adaptation in the face of scarcity, a culinary expression of life in the sertão (the arid scrublands of Brazil).

In the 18th century, carne seca production began in Rio Grande do Sul, taking advantage of the region's abundant supply of beef. The southern version of carne seca could last for over a year without spoiling. It contained more salt and underwent a more intense drying process under the sun and wind, earning the name charque. The charqueadas (drying yards) of Rio Grande do Sul began to distribute their products to consumer markets that had previously been supplied by the Northeast, including Rio de Janeiro, Bahia and Pernambuco.

Make your own carne de sol

Want to make your own carne de sol at home? It's easier than you think! Use tender cuts like rib-eye or filet mignon. For every 1kg (2¼lb) of meat, mix 150g (5¼oz) of salt with 30g (2 tablespoons) of light brown sugar. Cut the meat into steaks 2–3cm (¾–1¼in) thick. Rub the salt and sugar mixture evenly onto each piece, then wrap each piece in kitchen paper to absorb the moisture from the meat as it cures. Put all the wrapped pieces on a baking tray and refrigerate for 24 hours. Sear in a hot pan with a small amount of manteiga de garrafa or ghee until the steaks are cooked how you like them. Homemade carne de sol is still perishable once it's been cured, so store it in the fridge and consume within five to seven days after curing or freeze it.

This was the no. 1 best-seller when I had my café in Brazil. The exact origin of escondidinho is unknown, but it became especially popular in Pernambuco, Paraíba and Bahia. Think of it as Brazil's answer to shepherd's pie, only here, the ingredients are uniquely ours – a layer of hearty, flavourful dried beef topped with a creamy cassava mash – turning something familiar into something unmistakably Brazilian.

escondidinho de carne seca
Brazilian shepherd's pie

SERVES 4

FOR THE DRIED BEEF FILLING:
900g (2lb) carne seca (Brazilian dried beef)
30g (2 tbsp) butter
2 medium onions, finely chopped

FOR THE CASSAVA MASH:
800g (1¾lb) cassava, peeled and chopped, or frozen chopped cassava
250ml (1 cup) milk
110g (¼lb) butter
sea salt and freshly ground black pepper

FOR THE CHEESE LAYERS:
400g (1¾ cups) soft cheese, such as Catupiry or Requeijão, or cream cheese works well too
a handful of grated mozzarella or Parmesan cheese

Rinse the carne seca under cold running water, then soak it in cold water for at least 12 hours, changing the water every 3–4 hours. This method is ideal for carne seca imported from Brazil. If using carne seca produced elsewhere, it contains significantly less salt, so a 2-hour soak is sufficient.

Drain the beef and put it in a pot with fresh water. Bring to a boil, then reduce the heat to medium and cook until tender (about 40 minutes in a pressure cooker or 2 hours in a regular pot). Drain the water and shred the beef using two forks.

Melt the butter in a saucepan on a medium heat. Add the onions and cook for 5–8 minutes, until soft. Stir in the shredded beef and cook for a few more minutes. Check the seasoning and add some salt if necessary. Set aside.

To make the cassava mash, put the chopped cassava in a large pot, cover with cold water and bring to a boil. Reduce the heat and cook for 25–30 minutes, until soft. Drain and remove any fibrous strands from the centre of the cassava pieces. If using frozen chopped cassava, you can skip this step, as it typically doesn't contain fibrous strands.

Using a potato masher, mash the cooked cassava with the milk until smooth. Stir in the butter, then season with salt and pepper to taste. Mix well until creamy.

Preheat the oven to 180°C (350°F).

Spread the shredded beef filling evenly over the bottom of a 25cm (10in) square baking dish or a similar-sized casserole, then top the beef with the soft cheese. Finish with the cassava purée, spreading it smoothly. Add the grated mozzarella or Parmesan on top.

Bake in the preheated oven for 15–20 minutes, until heated through and slightly golden on top. Allow to stand for 5 minutes after removing from the oven, then use a big spoon to scoop out portions to serve.

The word 'jabá' comes from the Tupi-Guarani root word 'yupí', which means 'to flee' or 'fugitive'. According to historical accounts, Indigenous and enslaved people would carry salted, dried meat for sustenance during escapes. This was so prevalent that the meat itself became known as jabá.

The word 'jerimum' comes from the Tupi-Guarani word 'jari'rumu', which refers to squashes and pumpkins in general. Jerimum was part of the Indigenous diet and was the common term used by Indigenous people in Brazil long before Europeans arrived.

The combination of these two ingredients is a classic flavour pairing that works beautifully in many dishes, such as a filling for pastas, pies, pastéis (page 66) and more. Think ravioli filled with this beef and pumpkin mixture in a sage and butter sauce. Heaven!

jabá com jerimum
dried beef with pumpkin

SERVES 6

500g (18oz) carne seca (Brazilian dried beef), cut into large cubes

500g (18oz) pumpkin (jerimum) or butternut squash, peeled and diced

60ml (¼ cup) manteiga de garrafa (bottled butter) or ghee

2 medium onions, sliced

85g (3oz) biquinho peppers, whole or halved, or any pickled red peppers

4 spring onions, chopped

1 bunch of fresh coriander, chopped

sea salt and freshly ground black pepper

TO SERVE:

boiled white rice or farofa (page 33)

Rinse the carne seca under cold running water, then soak it in cold water for at least 12 hours, changing the water every 3–4 hours. This method is ideal for carne seca imported from Brazil. If using carne seca produced elsewhere, it contains significantly less salt, so a 2-hour soak is sufficient.

Drain the beef and put it in a pot with fresh water. Bring to a boil, then reduce the heat to medium and cook until tender (about 40 minutes in a pressure cooker or 2 hours in a regular pot). Drain and allow to cool, then remove any excess fat and shred the beef but keep the pieces chunky.

Cook the diced pumpkin or squash in a saucepan of boiling water until soft, then drain and set aside.

Warm the manteiga de garrafa or ghee in a large frying pan on a medium heat. Add the sliced onions and cook for 5–8 minutes, until soft. Add the shredded beef and stir for a few minutes to warm through, then add the cooked pumpkin, biquinho peppers, spring onions and fresh coriander. Stir gently to combine and heat everything evenly. Taste and adjust the salt if needed.

Serve hot with boiled white rice or farofa on the side.

biquinho peppers

Biquinho peppers are tiny, teardrop-shaped pods native to South America. First documented in Brazil, they are believed to have originated in the state of Minas Gerais. Today, biquinho peppers are popular both as ornamental plants in home gardens and as specialty crops grown on a small scale in Brazil, Peru and the United States.

These peppers are best known for their mild, sweet flavour and are most commonly enjoyed pickled. In Brazil, they're traditionally preserved in a mixture of vinegar, garlic and herbs, and served as a snack, condiment, edible garnish or in salads and stir-fries.

Paçoca originally comes from Indigenous food traditions. Toasted cassava flour would be blended with a protein (often dried meat or fish) by pounding them together, creating a nutrient-dense mixture. The name comes from the Tupi-Guarani word 'pa'soka', meaning 'to pound' or 'to crush'. This early paçoca contained little to no seasoning, maybe an occasional chilli. European settlers adapted the original recipe by adding salt (to improve flavour and preservation) and using carne seca. Thanks to its portability, nutritional value and long shelf life, this version of paçoca became a staple for the tropeiros, the travelling merchants, drovers and muleteers who travelled long distances across the country between the 17th and 19th centuries.

paçoca de carne seca
dried beef and cassava crumble

SERVES 2

200g (7oz) carne seca (Brazilian dried beef)

2 tbsp manteiga de garrafa (Brazilian bottled butter) or ghee

½ medium onion, diced

60g (½ cup) farinha de mandioca torrada (toasted cassava flour)

TO SERVE:

boiled white rice

cooked beans

fresh banana

Rinse the carne seca under cold running water, then soak it in cold water for at least 12 hours, changing the water every 3–4 hours. This method is ideal for carne seca imported from Brazil. If using carne seca produced elsewhere, it contains significantly less salt, so a 2-hour soak is sufficient.

Drain the beef and put it in a pot with fresh water. Bring to a boil, then reduce the heat to medium and cook until tender (about 40 minutes in a pressure cooker or 2 hours in a regular pot). Drain the water and shred the beef using two forks.

Warm the manteiga de garrafa or ghee in a frying pan on a medium heat. Add the diced onion and cook for 5–8 minutes, until soft. Add the shredded beef and stir to combine with the onion.

Transfer the mixture to a pilão (pestle and mortar). Add the toasted cassava flour and pound the mixture, pressing and mixing until it becomes well combined and slightly crumbly. If you don't have a pestle and mortar, you can use a blender or a food processor.

The best way to serve this dish is warm or at room temperature with boiled white rice, cooked beans and a fresh banana, but it also works well as a side.

paçoca de amendoim *peanut paçoca*

There's also a sweet version of paçoca, called paçoca de amendoim (peanut paçoca). This crumbly candy made from ground peanuts, sugar and a touch of cassava flour is a favourite in our house. The concept of mixing cassava flour with other ingredients was adapted by colonists, who introduced sugar into the recipe. Peanuts combined with sugar provided a high-energy, non-perishable food, much like the original meat dish. By swapping carne seca for ground peanuts, it created the sweet paçoca we know today.

To make the sweet version, put 250g (about 1¾ cups) skinned, roasted, unsalted peanuts in a food processor or blender with 200g (1 cup) caster sugar, 30g (¼ cup) toasted or untoasted cassava flour (or you can use cornflakes) and ½ teaspoon salt. Blend for about 5 minutes, until the mixture is finely ground – almost to a paste – and evenly combined.

Press the mixture into round moulds or shape it by hand, packing it firmly. You can use anything that you have at home – for example, an espresso cup will give a nice shape. You should get around 18 x 30g (1oz) portions. Unmould and serve, no baking required!

sugarcane

our sweet heritage

Brazil isn't just the largest producer of sugarcane in the world, we're also the sweetest people! From the conventual sweets of Portuguese monasteries to our obsession with condensed milk and the unique cachaça, sugar has shaped our history, economy and identity. But behind every spoonful of sweetness, there's a story of power, labour and land.

The decline of Portugal's lucrative spice trade with India played a key role in the decision to colonise Brazil, and sugarcane quickly emerged as the most strategic economic substitute, becoming the new pillar of their wealth. Portugal already had experience cultivating and processing sugar in its Atlantic Island territories, such as Madeira and the Azores, where essential techniques had been developed.

However, by the early 16th century, the Portuguese nobility had been weakened by the collapse of Eastern trade and lacked the resources to finance large-scale sugar production in Brazil. This gap created an opportunity for the emerging merchant class to step in. With their capital and organisational know-how, they played a central role in establishing Brazil's sugar economy, financing plantations (engenhos), importing enslaved labour and structuring a transatlantic trade system that shaped the colony for centuries.

The rise of sugarcane production in Brazil drove the expansion of colonial settlements, pushing the boundaries of exploration and development into new regions. But perhaps the most lasting legacy of sugarcane production is the deep inequality that still shapes Brazilian society today.

On the cooking side of history, sugar transformed our tables and redefined the act of eating. Unlike Indigenous and African traditions, where food was primarily for survival, the Portuguese introduced the idea of eating for pleasure – savouring something just because you wanted to, not because you needed to. Portuguese women played a central role in this shift, turning local ingredients into refined delicacies. Almonds gave way to peanuts or coconut, while figs and marmalades were replaced by tropical fruits like cashews and passion fruit. Sugar introduced a new kind of cuisine, one rooted in leisure, preservation and social ritual.

Brazilians are famously known for loving desserts that are very sweet, but our classic pause for coffee and something sweet is still deeply rooted in our culture, our habits and our daily rhythm. We inherited this delicious social ritual from the Portuguese. From the afternoon cakes our grandmothers used to bake to the famous bolinho com café (a small piece of cake and black coffee), it's never been just about the cake. It's a reason to pause, to gather, to share stories. Sharing a sweet is a human connection, wrapped in sugar.

There's no samba without caipirinha, and no caipirinha without samba. I love caipirinha so much that it was the one thing I truly craved after giving birth to my son. A year and a half later, once I finished breastfeeding, that first sip tasted absolutely delightful.

Caipirinha is more than a cocktail – it's part of our cultural heritage. Its origins are often traced back to a home remedy from the Alentejo region of Portugal, where a mixture of aguardente from sugarcane, lemon, garlic and honey was used to treat patients suffering from the Spanish flu.

At some point, someone (thankfully!) decided to skip the garlic and honey, added a few spoonfuls of sugar to tame the acidity of the lime and tossed in some ice to cool things down. And just like that, the caipirinha was born.

The drink as we know it today was invented by landowning farmers in Piracicaba, in the interior of São Paulo, during the 19th century. Originally served at upscale events and parties, it quickly became a national favourite. The name 'caipirinha' is the diminutive of 'Caipira', a term that refers to people from rural São Paulo.

caipirinha

MAKES 1

½ lime, sliced
2½ tbsp caster sugar (or brown sugar, honey or any other sweetener)
60ml (¼ cup) cachaça
ice cubes

variation

You can use other fruits that are just as delicious as the traditional lime. Try strawberries, passion fruit, cashew fruit (the fruit, not the nuts) or pineapple.

Put the lime slices in a sturdy glass and sprinkle the sugar over them. Using a muddler, gently press the centre of each slice to release its juice. Avoid over-muddling to prevent bitterness from the rind leaching into the drink.

Pour in the cachaça and stir well to combine with the lime and sugar. Add the ice cubes and give it one last stir. Serve immediately.

A Brazilian birthday party without brigadeiro is not a birthday party. But don't be fooled by the charm of these beloved little chocolate balls. We have a whole line-up of other party sweets that are just as tasty. Beijinho (which means 'little kiss', how cute is that?), made with desiccated coconut and condensed milk, comes in a close second. Then there's bicho de pé, olho de sogra (mother-in-law eyes – don't ask!) and cajuzinho. Sure, there are newer, trendier flavours out there, but I'm loyal to the old-school ones I grew up with. The real star in all these sweets is condensed milk. We Brazilians are famous – maybe notorious – for using it in nearly every dessert.

Brazilian birthday party sweets

beijinho

1 x 397g (14oz) tin of condensed milk

15g (1 tbsp) butter

1 tinful of double cream (after emptying the condensed milk, use the tin to measure the cream)

100g (1⅓ cups) desiccated coconut, plus extra for coating

brigadeiro

1 x 397g (14oz) tin of condensed milk

15g (1 tbsp) butter

1 tinful of double cream (after emptying the condensed milk, use the tin to measure the cream)

30g (⅓ cup) unsweetened cocoa power

chocolate sprinkles, for coating

cajuzinho

1 x 397g (14oz) tin of condensed milk

15g (1 tbsp) butter

150g (1 cup) peanuts, finely chopped

caster sugar, for coating

bicho de pé
(strawberry sweets)

1 x 395g (14oz) tin of condensed milk

15g (1 tbsp) butter

60g (½ cup) Nesquik strawberry milk powder

caster sugar, for coating

olho de sogra

Use the same recipe for the beijinho. Take a pitted prune and gently open it into a little cup, then fill it with a small ball of beijinho. This creates the look of an eye with contrasting colours. Finally, roll it in granulated sugar and put in a small paper cup.

For all variations, you start the same way: put the condensed milk, butter, cream (if using) and your chosen flavour in a saucepan on a medium heat and gently warm. If your recipe includes cream, it will take a bit longer, and it might bubble up and try to escape the pot. Use a high-sided pan unless you want your stove to look like a sweet crime scene.

How do you know it's ready? After it's been cooking for about 20 minutes and you can see the bottom of the pan as you stir, set the timer for 3–5 minutes and don't stop stirring. Ever. The mixture should thicken and pull away cleanly from the sides.

Once done, pour the mixture onto a plate or baking tray and let it cool completely before rolling into balls. There is no right or wrong when it comes to the size, though the size of your paper cups will determine that. If you're making the cajuzinho, form it into the shape of a large cashew nut and add a peanut on top. I like to make my sweets about the size of a walnut so that you have a good balance of crunchy coating and creamy filling.

Roll the balls in caster sugar, then put each one in a mini cupcake cup to serve. These will last in an airtight container at room temperature for up to two weeks.

tips & twists

Bottom line? All you need is condensed milk + butter + whatever flavour you fancy!

1. You can swap heavy cream for whole milk or any full-fat dairy – just not skimmed milk.

2. You can also skip milk altogether in any recipe: condensed milk + butter + cocoa powder is a classic combo.

3. No cocoa powder? Use dark chocolate (70% or whatever darkness matches your mood).

4. Use apricots instead of prunes for the olho de sogra.

5. Replace the strawberry milk powder with strawberry gelatine or freeze-dried fruits for a more grown-up vibe.

6. Other flavour ideas: passion fruit juice, lemon zest, pineapple + coconut (hello, piña colada!) or even cinnamon all work well.

7. White brigadeiro? Yes, you can! Use white chocolate instead of cocoa (and skip the butter).

8. Cajuzinho means 'little cashew', but it's only just occurred to me that this recipe usually uses peanuts. But why not use cashews? The choice is yours!

Whenever I went to the farmers' market with my grandma, we would always end up at the pastel stall, so I had to find a way to sneak pastel into this book. There's no sugar in this recipe, so you might be wondering what it's doing in the sugarcane chapter. Here's my excuse: pastel often includes cachaça, which comes from sugarcane. And when you consider that pastel is frequently served with garapa (sugarcane juice), suddenly this doesn't feel like a loophole – it was meant to be.

The pastel as we know it in Brazil today originated in the 1940s with the descendants of Japanese immigrants in Santos, São Paulo. It was inspired by Chinese spring rolls and Japanese gyoza but adapted with local ingredients, like swapping cachaça for sake.

According to some accounts, Japanese immigrants in Brazil faced discrimination during World War Two. (Did you know that São Paulo contains the largest concentration of Japanese people outside of Japan?) To avoid it, they opened pastel shops while passing themselves off as Chinese. The recipe quickly spread throughout São Paulo and became one of the state's most popular street foods, sold both in open-air markets and pastel shops. By the 1950s, the tradition of eating pastel had reached Rio de Janeiro and Belo Horizonte, solidifying its place in Brazilian food culture.

pastel
fried pastry

MAKES 16

690g (5¾ cups) plain flour

5 tbsp vegetable oil

1½ tbsp cachaça (Brazilian sugarcane liquor)

1 tbsp salt

280ml (1 cup + 2 tbsp) water

your chosen filling (see the opposite page)

vegetable oil, for deep-frying

Put the flour on a clean countertop in a mound. Make a well in the centre and add the oil, cachaça and salt. Gradually add the water while using your fingertips to mix the liquid ingredients with the flour, incorporating a little at a time until it's all combined into a smooth, uniform dough.

Cover the dough with a clean cloth or put it inside a plastic bag to prevent it from drying out. Let it rest for 30 minutes.

Divide the dough in half. Using a rolling pin, roll out each portion into a paper-thin sheet. The thinner the dough, the crispier the pastel will be when fried. No extra flour is needed for rolling.

Cut the dough into 16cm (6¼in) squares. Add 1 generous tablespoon (a mom tablespoon, as we say in Brazil!) of your filling in the centre of each square. Be careful not to overfill, or the pastries might burst open while frying. After filling,

brush the edges of the dough with water, then fold each one in half to form a rectangle. Seal the edges by pressing them together with the tines of a fork.

Heat the oil in a deep-fryer to 180°C–190°C (350°F–375°F). If you don't have a deep-fryer, fill a high-sided saucepan no more than half full of oil. Line a baking tray with kitchen paper, then set a wire rack on top.

Working in batches, add a few pastéis and fry for 2–3 minutes, flipping them over halfway through the cooking time, until they are golden and crispy. Tip out onto the wire rack to let any excess oil drain off while you cook the rest.

Pastéis are best enjoyed while they're still warm and crispy with a glass of sugarcane juice, a classic Brazilian combination.

filling combos

1. **CHEESE:** Simply filled with grated mozzarella.

2. **PIZZA:** Grated mozzarella, diced tomatoes and a pinch of oregano.

3. **BEEF AND EGG:** Seasoned, cooked beef mince with chopped hard-boiled egg.

4. **BEEF AND CHEESE:** Cooked beef mince and grated cheese.

5. **SHRIMP (CAMARÃO):** Use the smallest shrimp you can find. You can use them raw, just make sure they're well-seasoned. If you're using larger shrimp, cook them first and season well before using as a filling.

6. **DRIED BEEF WITH PUMPKIN:** While not a classic combo, try the recipe on page 56 as a pastel filling.

Blasta Books

an imprint of Nine Bean Rows

23 Mountjoy Square

Dublin, D01 E0F8

Ireland

@blastabooks

blastabooks.com

First published 2026

001

© Giselle Makinde, 2026

ISBN: 978-1-0684050-2-0

Editor: Kristin Jensen

Designer: Jane Matthews

Photographer: Jo Murphy

Food stylist: Charlotte O'Connell

Cover illustrator: Ella Ginn

Proofreader: Jocelyn Doyle

Printed by L&C Printing Group, Poland

This product is made of material from well-managed, FSC®-certified forests and other controlled sources.

All rights reserved.

No part of this publication may be copied, reproduced or transmitted in any form or by any means without written permission of the publishers.

A CIP catalogue record for this book is available from the British Library.

For EU product safety concerns, contact info@ninebeanrowsbooks.com.

about the author

Giselle Makinde is a chef and storyteller who believes food can bring people and cultures together. She was born and raised in Brazil, and like the dishes she cooks, she's a mix of many influences: Portuguese, African and Indigenous. She is proud of that blend, and it influences everything she does.

Giselle has been working as a chef for over 25 years, but her journey started at home, in her mother's kitchen. When she moved to Ireland, Giselle started thinking more about sustainability and how we use food. That's what led her to create Cream of the Crop, a gelato company that turned surplus ingredients into something delicious and saved more than 50 tons of food from going to waste. Giselle closed the company after four years to make space for new challenges, but preventing food waste and rethinking how we eat remain at the core of her work, which is always rooted in the flavours of her childhood.

@sambabygiselle